# Hans Christian Andersen's
# THE UGLY
# DUCKLING

## Retold and Illustrated by
## IAN BECK

ORCHARD BOOKS

Once upon a time there was a mother duck, who had seven little ducklings. Six of them were soft and fluffy and yellow, and said, "Quack."

The seventh duckling was quite different. He was grey and spiky and had a long neck, and could only say, "Honk."

The other ducklings called him 'ugly'.
He tried hard to be liked, but the other
ducklings never played with him.

His mother would shake her head. "Quack. Are you sure you are mine?" she said. "Quack, you're a funny sort of duck."

One day they all swam over to visit the ducks on the other side of the river. The ugly duckling, as always, followed far behind.

The other big ducks hissed and pecked at him. "Go away," they quacked. "We don't like you; you're not much of a duck."

But "Honk," was all the sad little duckling could say.

That night as the other ducks slept, the ugly
duckling swam far away and hid in some reeds
by a pond. "Honk, no one wants me," he sniffed.
An old cat came prowling along, "Miaow,
what sort of bird are you?" she asked.

"I'm a duckling, honk," replied the ugly duckling.

"Mmmm, miaow, funny sort of duck," said the cat, and she crept off to hunt for mice.

The weather grew colder, but the ugly duckling stayed all alone by the little pond.

One bright day, he saw some beautiful white birds with long necks, flying high overhead. "Honk," he called out to them, "where are you going?"

"Far away south, where it's warm," they called back. "Come fly with us."

The ugly duckling skittered across the water.
"Wait for me!" he honked. But he wasn't ready
to fly yet, and the white birds flew on far far away.

Before long winter came. Snow fell and there was ice on the pond. The ugly duckling had no mother to snuggle up against and keep warm.

"Honk," he said to himself, "I'm so unhappy."

Then one bright morning he woke up to find the snow and ice had melted, and the world was green again. Feeling strong, he tried his wings. They had grown through the winter, and he soared up easily from the pond into the clear blue sky.

"Honk," he cried in excitement. "Honk, honk!"
He flew on over the land, following the shape
of the big river in the spring sunshine.

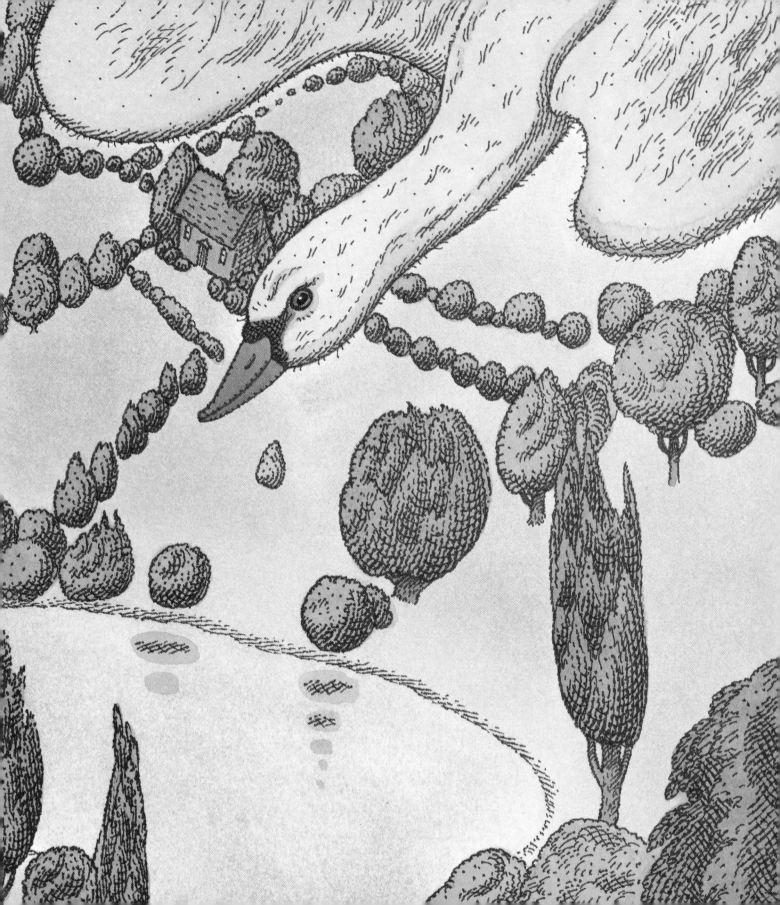

Soon the days grew longer and warmer, for summer had come. One day he saw the beautiful white birds again. The ugly duckling flew down and landed near them on the shimmering water.

"Honk," said the beautiful birds. "Hello, come
and swim with us here. There's plenty to eat,"
and they plunged their long necks into the water.

"Honk, who me?" said the ugly duckling.
"Swim with you? But I'm just an ugly duckling;
no one wants me."

The white birds all laughed. "You're not ugly, and you're not a duckling at all," they said. "You are a young swan, just like us. Look at yourself in the water... and you will see."

The ugly duckling looked down into the water and saw his own reflection.

His feathers were now a brilliant white all over, he had a long neck, and a bright gold and black beak. He was a swan just like the others.

He honked happily, it didn't matter now that he couldn't quack.

The swans gathered around him. "Welcome," they said.

So the once ugly duckling, who had grown into
a beautiful swan, flew away with the other swans over
the blue water, and lived happily ever after.

"Honk, honk!"